TAKING ECONOMICS SERIOUSLY

TAKING
ECONOMICS
SERIOUSLY

Dean Baker

A Boston Review Book

THE MIT PRESS Cambridge, Mass. London, England

MIT Press books may be purchased at special quantity
discounts for business or sales promotional use. For
information, please e-mail special_sales@mitpress.mit.edu or
write to Special Sales Department, The MIT Press,
55 Hayward Street, Cambridge, MA 02142.

This book was set in Adobe Garamond by *Boston Review*
and was printed and bound in the United States of America.

Library of Congress Cataloging-in-Publication Data
Baker, Dean, 1958–
  Taking economics seriously / Dean Baker.
      p. cm.
  "A Boston Review Book."
  ISBN 978-0-262-01418-2 (hbk. : alk. paper) 1. Economics
I. Title.
  HB171.B22 2010
  330—dc22

                                        2009052072

10   9   8   7   6   5   4   3   2   1

Dedicated to the hope that we can start thinking about economic policy in ways that do not always work to the advantage of the rich and powerful.

CONTENTS

1

The Myth of the Free Market

THE EXTRAORDINARY FINANCIAL COL-
lapse of 2008 is commonly described as a
testament to the failure of deregulation. The
events are indeed testament to a failure—a
failure of public policy. Blaming deregulation is misleading.

In general, political debates over regulation have been wrongly cast as disputes over
the extent of regulation, with conservatives
assumed to prefer less regulation, while liberals prefer more. In fact conservatives do
not necessarily desire less regulation, nor do
liberals necessarily desire more. Conserva-

tives support regulatory structures that cause income to flow upward, while liberals support regulatory structures that promote equality. "Less" regulation does not imply greater inequality, nor is the reverse true.

Framing regulation debates in terms of more and less is not only inaccurate. It also biases the argument toward conservative positions by characterizing an extremely intrusive structure of regulation—for example, patent and copyright rules—as the free market. In the realm of insurance and finance over the last two decades, calls for deregulation have been cover for rules tilted starkly toward corporate interests. And the recent change in bankruptcy law, hailed by conservatives, requires much greater government involvement in the economy. In the health care debates, too, invasive regulatory structures have led even economists to overlook their own basic principles, giving corporate interests huge advantages. In the U.S. economy, there is no free market. It is just that structures that heavily regulate the economy are taken as inevitable.

False ideological claims have, thus, circumscribed the public debate over regulation and blinded us to the wide range of choices we have. Without these claims, what would guide regulatory policy? What kinds of choices would we make? In this book, I explore what shifting the terms of debate might gain us.

CONSIDER PATENT AND COPYRIGHT PROtection. We cannot have a serious discussion of the relative merits of patents and copyrights until we recognize that these are public policies rather than intrinsic features of the free market. Debates about both patent and copyright have been hugely distorted by the failure to recognize this obvious fact.

It does not matter that we call patents and copyrights "property" or even that we have a clause in the Constitution that authorizes Congress to grant patents and copyrights. Suppose autoworkers were given a property right to a job in the automobile industry, a right they could even sell. Would anyone say that this right to a job is part of the free market?

Patents and copyrights are government-granted protections designed for a specific public purpose, as stated in the Constitution: "to promote the Progress of Science and useful Arts." But granting intellectual property rights is one of many possible mechanisms for accomplishing this important goal. Whether patents and copyrights are the most effective mechanisms for the promotion of the arts and sciences is an empirical question. And the answer could be different depending on social and economic circumstances. These particular mechanisms also necessitate enforcement regimes, generating substantial economic waste.

Consider the situation with copyrights (I discuss patents in detail in Chapter 2). In the Internet age, almost any printed or recorded material—music, movies, books, video games—can be instantly transferred anywhere in the world at almost no cost. However, rather than allowing the public to enjoy the full benefit of this technology, the government has created a dizzying array of new laws and restrictions designed to make it more difficult, and legally more risky, to pass along material that is subject to copyright protection.

To preserve copyright, the government has imposed an aggressive sanction regime even on seemingly minor offenders. In one case, a woman in Minnesota faced a fine of more than $200,000 for allowing people to download music from her computer. Universities have been told to police dorm rooms to ensure that students are not downloading material in violation of copyright, and administrations have been encouraged to conduct classes teaching that it is wrong to make unauthorized copies of copyrighted material.

The government has repeatedly prohibited the production of various types of hardware until protections could be installed to prevent the duplication of copyrighted material. It has banned the development of software that can break through copyright protections. In one well-known incident, a Russian computer scientist, Dmitry Sklyarov, was arrested by the FBI after a conference presentation in which he described a way to get around a form of copyright protection.

The list of extraordinary government measures that have been developed to enhance copyright protection is lengthy. Remarkably, these measures are never described as forms of government regulation. They are treated as enforcement measures necessary to protect copyright. However, a government-granted monopoly with extensive rules and heavy-handed enforcement is not the only way to promote creativity.

A vast amount of creative and artistic work is already supported through mechanisms that do not depend on copyright protection. Private foundations are a major alternative source of support, as are the limited funds available through public programs such as the National Endowments for the Arts and Humanities. Colleges and universities are probably the largest source of funding not dependent on copyright. Professors are expected to research and write in addition to their teaching responsibilities.

It is easy to envision mechanisms to expand support for creative and artistic work outside the copyright regime. For example, it would be possible to design a tax credit for individuals who either support creative work directly or contribute to organizations that support such work. The credit could be modeled after the tax deduction for nonprofits or charities. Even a modest tax credit (e.g., $100 per person)—which taxpayers could allocate to an artist, writer, musician, or film producer of their choice—would likely be sufficient to fund almost all of the work currently supported by the copyright system.

Alternatives to copyright are feasible and probably far more efficient than the copyright system. And they would replace a gigantic array of enforcement measures that can themselves be seen as unnecessary forms of government intervention in the economy.

Another example of excessive government regulation, never discussed as such, is the bankruptcy-reform bill that passed Congress in 2005. This bill substantially strengthened the conditions imposed on people seeking bankruptcy protection, making such protection a much less attractive option.

This bankruptcy bill undoubtedly resonated with those inclined to accept that people succeed or fail largely as a result of their own actions, but, most importantly, it obscured the real issue that the bill addressed: to what lengths should the government go to collect unpaid bills? The party seeking the aid of the government in this story was the creditor, not the debtor.

The new law hugely expanded the creditors' claims on future earnings. This means that the government is now far more involved in bill collection than it used to be, possibly monitoring the wages of millions of individuals in bankruptcy who still have debts to creditors. (For those who worry about the negative incentives caused by taxation, it is worth noting that having money deducted from paychecks to pay creditors provides the same disincentive to work.)

There are many other cases of excessive government regulation, never discussed as such, in which the conservative position arguably requires more government involvement in the economy than the liberal position. For years ice cream–makers Ben and Jerry's Homemade has fought attempts by state governments to ban labeling dairy products as free of recombinant bovine growth hormone (rBGH). Some pressure groups associated with the dairy industry argue that the rBGH-free label implies that bovine growth hormones are harmful, which has not been established by the Food and Drug Administration. Of course, Ben and Jerry's Homemade is not trying to prevent its competitors from assuring the public that their ice cream is safe. It is trying to make a truthful claim about its own ice cream.

In the same vein, the Department of Agriculture (USDA) recently prohibited a meatpacker from testing its cattle for mad cow disease. The meatpacker had intended to privately test all of its cattle, whereas the USDA tests only 1 percent of cattle. But the USDA, arguing that full testing would cause the public to question the safety of other meat, moved to prevent it.

Deregulation can be a principled position held by true believers in a free market. But, to be fair, rarely does either side argue against regulation as such. The real issue is the structure of regulation and its impact on economic outcomes, especially income distribution.

In the decades preceding the financial collapse, for example, regulations designed to protect the public and ensure the stability of the financial system were considerably weakened, but the system was (and is) quite far from being deregulated.

Wall Streeters wanted one-sided regulation that provided them with an enormous government security blanket—the too-big-to-fail (TBTF) principle—without any costs or conditions. None of the Citigroup, Goldman Sachs, J.P. Morgan crew ever lobbied Congress for an explicit repeal of TBTF. And while many on Wall Street lost their jobs when the bubble burst, the tens or hundreds of millions of dollars that banking executives earned during the good times are theirs to keep. Even with the market collapse, the vast majority of them are almost certainly better off than they would have been had they done honest work over the last decade.

IF THE REAL DEBATE IS OVER THE TYPE rather than extent of regulation, then why is it always framed as the latter? For conservatives, the answer is obvious. Many Americans embrace the idea of free markets and hold a deep aversion to government. Faith in government ebbs and flows, even in the most liberal times. It will almost always be advantageous, then, to associate a political position with support of the free market.

It is less apparent why liberals would be so eager to accept such a harmful caricature of their position. The answer requires digging a bit deeper into what their position implies about the nature of the economy and economic outcomes.

Like conservatives, liberals generally acknowledge that people get ahead as a result of their skills and hard work, with some luck thrown in. The main difference in the liberal and conservative views of the economy is that liberals are more likely to believe that many people face serious impediments to their success and do not get the same chance as people from wealthier backgrounds. Liberals are also likely to feel guilty about the difference in opportunities and therefore support political measures that will reduce the gap and help those at the bottom. However, most liberals still accept the proposition that the distribution of income is fundamentally determined by the market rather than political decisions embodied in regulations such as patents, copyrights, and bankruptcy law.

But what if we accept a view that virtually every facet of the economy is shaped by policies that could easily be altered? Investment bankers get incredibly rich because the government gives them the shelter of TBTF but does not impose any serious prudential regulation in return. Bill Gates gets incredibly rich because, through copyright and patents, the government gives him a monopoly on the operating system that is (or was) used by 90 percent of the computers in the world.

Doctors are well paid because, unlike less politically connected workers, they enjoy protection from international competition. The same is true for lawyers and other highly paid professionals. Their high salaries depend less on skill and hard work than on being able to structure labor markets in ways that autoworkers, textile workers, and cab drivers cannot.

There is a long list of professional licensing requirements—many of which have nothing to do with maintaining standards of quality—that make it difficult for foreign professionals to work in the United States. While trade pacts such as the North American Free Trade Agreement have been designed explicitly to eliminate institutional barriers that obstruct investment in developing countries and the free flow of manufactured goods back into the United States, there has been no comparable effort to reduce or eliminate the barriers that obstruct highly educated professionals in the developing world from practicing their professions in the United States. Many ambitious professionals from the developing world do manage to overcome these barriers, but professionals in the United States still enjoy a far greater level of protection from international competition than less highly educated workers.

THE LESS-VERSUS-MORE FRAMING OF REGulation supports the premise that there is in principle an unregulated market out there and that some of us wish to rein in this unregulated market while others would leave it alone. This is consistent with the idea that large inequalities in income distribution just happen as a result of market forces. But as the above examples illustrate, no one is really talking about an unregulated market—rather, we are all just talking about whom the regulation is designed to benefit. Distribution of income has never preceded the intervention of government.

The government is always present, steering the benefits in different directions depending on who is in charge. Accepting this view provides a political vantage point much better suited to the case for progressive regulation. After all, conservatives want the big hand of government in the market as well. They just want the handouts all to go to those at the top.

This expansive view of regulation puts everything up for grabs, including the hefty salaries of many of those arguing the liberal position. Do liberals really want everyone asking if we can have the same economic benefits by removing trade barriers in physicians' and lawyers' services that we gain by removing barriers to clothes and cars? Liberals, too, are invested in the obfuscation that less-versus-more provides.

Even so, the catastrophe produced by the one-sided deregulation of the financial industry, coupled with a long list of regulatory failures in other areas, will almost certainly lead to a serious rethinking of regulatory policy in the years ahead. It remains to be seen whether this rethinking will go beyond the familiar debate. We know that when we emerge from the current crisis the economy will be extensively regulated. The questions is, to whose benefit? If we return to fundamentals, we see that we have a choice.

2

Malpractice

FUNDAMENTAL ECONOMIC PRINCIPLES tell us that goods should be sold at their marginal cost of production—the cost of producing one more unit of the good. If a company needs to pay twenty dollars for the material and labor used to produce one more shirt, then shirts should sell for twenty dollars plus a small profit-earning markup. The price-equals-marginal-cost principle maximizes economic efficiency and limits opportunities for fraud and corruption. Building on this principle, economists also strongly advocate globalization: the elimination of trade barriers allows consumers to buy goods and services from where they are cheapest, thus maximizing global efficiency and output.

Unfortunately, when it comes to health care, these principles are routinely violated. Certainly there was little discussion in the 2009 health care debate about redesigning the system so that prices were closer to marginal cost. The power of corporate interests was so great, and the current thinking so deeply entrenched, that there was almost no serious consideration of the implications of this basic economic principle for the health care sector.

Prescription drugs that could be manufactured and sold profitably for a few dollars per prescription may instead sell for thousands. Performing one more high-tech scan or other medical test may require just a few cents of electricity and a couple of hundred dollars worth of a technician's or a doctor's time. But diagnostic procedures can be billed at several thousand dollars a shot. Prices are often well above marginal costs, yet economists involved in health care reform rarely recognize this as a problem.

Nor do they show their usual zeal for trade. Health care may have features that make it place-specific, but globalization offers clear opportunities for gains. Specifically, the health care system can take greater advantage of foreign doctors and highly skilled medical professionals, who can be trained at far lower cost in the developing world than in the United States. And it is simple to design mechanisms that increase the number of trained personnel by an amount sufficient to supply both the United States and developing countries with more doctors and health care professionals. We should also consider that globalization offers people ways to get health care where it is cheaper, which is already happening to some extent with the growth of medical tourism.

Too-often ignored, the basic economic principles of marginal-cost pricing and gains from trade have much to offer in the area of health care. They need to be brought into the discussion.

Suppose a family member is diagnosed with a rare and typically fatal form of cancer. She is 80 years old and in otherwise good health. A drug with no major side effects but an uncertain success rate costs $200,000 for a year's dosage (the actual price for some newly developed cancer drugs). Should the family struggle to come up with money for the treatment, or alternatively, should an insurance company or the government be forced to pick up the tab? Should treatment be withheld?

This question has no good answers. The decision to allow a loved one to die when a possible cure exists would haunt the family for years to come. However, as individuals and as a society, we know that what we can spend on health care has limits. Suppose we spend the $200,000 and the patient dies anyway in 6 months. Is that a good use of money—ours or anyone's—in a world where poor children are going without decent housing, child care, or even food everyday?

Now change the story slightly. A year's dosage costs $200, and the calculation becomes suddenly far less difficult. With a reasonable hope of benefit, we would, of course, expect an insurance company or the government to pick up the tab, if it is not paid out-of-pocket.

Reducing the price to $200 is neither slight of hand, nor wishful thinking; it is marginal-cost pricing. Brand drugs, selling at hundreds or thousands of dollars per prescription, are not chemically distinct from the ones on Wal-Mart's shelves for four dollars. Few drugs are expensive to manufacture and distribute. A year's dosage of a cancer drug sells for $200,000 because the government grants the drug's developer a patent monopoly as an incentive to develop new drugs. Without that monopoly, the latest drug could be one of thousands of low-priced generics.

Economics textbooks are filled with graphs showing how trade barriers that raise the price of shirts or shoes by 10-20 percent above marginal cost lead to economic inefficiency and make the economy as a whole less productive. The same graphs would show large losses when government patent protections drive drug and medical-equipment prices above marginal costs—on the order of 1,000 percent, 10,000 percent, and in some cases 100,000 percent. Some cancer drugs, such as Avastin and Erbitux, are particularly overpriced.

Even in Econ 101, though, the direct inefficiency associated with setting prices above marginal cost is only part of the story. When government interference sets the price of any product above its marginal cost, it also creates the opportunity for monopoly rents—extra profits due to artificial scarcity. The rents cause producers to engage in wasteful activities that will maximize the value of their share of excess profits. These activities include lobbying politicians, pursuing expensive legal actions, advertising and marketing, and in the cases of prescription drugs and medical equipment and supplies, possibly withholding relevant data on effectiveness and safety. As economic theory predicts, all of these forms of rent-seeking thrive in abundance in the pharmaceutical and medical-supply industries.

The pharmaceutical industry always invests heavily in political campaigns: no surprise, since government actions directly affect its profitability. For example, the Medicare Modernization Act, which created the Medicare prescription drug benefit, was largely crafted to meet the needs of the pharmaceutical industry. Almost immediately after the passage of the bill, Representative Billy Tauzin, who was Chair of the House Energy and Commerce Committee, became president of Pharmaceutical Research and Manufacturers of America, the industry lobbying group, a reward for his work in getting the bill to the House floor.

The industry also regularly fights about the length and depth of its patents. Extending the length or increasing the strength of patent protection can mean large increases in profits. And companies work to ensure easy (and ideally costless) access to research funded by taxpayers through the National Institutes of Health (NIH) or other public institutions. In addition, the industry counts on the U.S. government to represent it in dealing with foreign countries. Measures that strengthen foreign commitments to protect drug patents feature prominently in almost every trade pact negotiated over the last two decades.

The pharmaceutical industry can expect substantial returns on its investments in political influence at the state level, where decisions are made about which drugs will be covered by Medicaid and other state programs. In addition to the direct demand generated by extending state Medicaid coverage to a new drug, the practices of state Medicaid programs in covering drugs help to build pressure on private insurers, so that they will also cover the drug for their patients.

The industry can expect returns from legal actions to enforce or extend patent protection as well. Brand-name drug companies commonly initiate suits against producers of generics even when those producers enter a market after a patent has expired. The brand producer generally has a basis for getting into court since there will often be at least some colorable claim to patent infringement. (There are typically many patents that apply to a particular drug.) But there is enormous asymmetry in potential gains for both parties. The brand manufacturer is securing its right to sell its product at a patent-protected price, and the generic producer is trying to gain the right to sell drugs in a competitive market. As a result, a producer of generics will often make concessions simply to be left alone. In some cases, it may surrender the right to compete altogether, deciding that potential profits will not offset the cost of the legal proceedings. The brand manufacturers have very deep pockets.

And the rent-seeking does not end with lobbying and legal bullying. It is hardly a secret that pharmaceutical companies find extensive advertising and marketing campaigns profitable. The industry spends almost as much on advertising and marketing as it does on research. Its ads dominate commercial breaks on news shows, encouraging viewers to ask their doctors about drugs for arthritis, heart disease, and many other common ailments. Patients cannot assess the merits of a particular drug based on a commercial pitch, but the industry hopes that doctors will prescribe the drug if patients ask for it. This route is not likely to lead to the best medical outcomes.

The other part of the industry's marketing effort is the work of the detailers, the tens of thousands of ground workers who go from doctor's office to doctor's office pitching the latest drugs. Ostensibly, they provide doctors important information about new drugs. In reality, they often have little knowledge of the drugs and are hired for being effective salespeople. In fact, the industry has made a strategy of seeking out former cheerleaders because they are generally attractive and can be enthusiastic promoters.

Perhaps the most pernicious form of drug-industry rent-seeking occurs when companies conceal research findings that reflect poorly on their drugs. The industry maintains control of its research and only shares results that it considers appropriate to make public. (The Food and Drug Administration is prohibited from revealing the results of any studies the industry makes available to it, but evidence is occasionally leaked by researchers concerned about the public's health.) A regular flow of news stories report concealed research findings suggesting that certain drugs could be harmful or ineffective. *The Washington Post*, for example, reported last year that the schizophrenia drug Seroquel may be less effective than claimed. Studies revealing the potentially harmful effects of the arthritis drug Vioxx were famously suppressed. Given the enormous profits at stake, the withholding of relevant evidence from drug research is entirely predictable.

While few economists would dispute that patent monopolies in pharmaceuticals and medical technology provide incentives for wasteful activities, they defend patents as the price we must pay for financing drug research and development. But patents are simply one option for financing research, not essential at all. We could expand the public funding going to NIH or other public institutions and extend their charge beyond basic research to include developing and testing drugs and medical equipment. Or the government could contract out the research and development process to private firms and pay for the work up front so that all patentable results fall in the public domain. Or the government could construct a prize mechanism under which it buys up patents after the fact for a premium keyed to the patent's usefulness.

The government will need to provide funding to cover research costs through whatever mechanism of public financing is chosen, but this expense is likely to be dwarfed by the savings from marginal-cost pricing for prescription drugs. The amount of patent-supported research that must be replaced would be in the neighborhood of $30 billion a year, while the savings from marginal-cost pricing would almost certainly be more than $200 billion a year. The difference now goes to marketing costs and profits. While generic makers would still make normal profits on their sales, brand company profits would be far lower if research were funded by the government.

Public funding obviously involves the government in research, but demand for medical care is already determined in large part through the political process. The vast majority of health care costs are paid by third parties, either insurance companies or the government; costs are not distributed according to individuals' willingness to pay. If the government and insurance companies cannot be forced to pay for a drug, the industry will not develop it. Since politics inevitably decide which drugs are developed, government and insurance companies should determine whether they will pay for a drug *before* it is developed. This way there is no painful question about whether to spend $200,000 on a year's dose for our 80-year-old loved one. Though the ethical calculus is similar, it is much easier to forgo hundreds of millions of dollars researching a drug that may benefit relatively few, hypothetical people than to refuse $200,000 for a drug that may benefit a real dying person.

The logic of paying for research upfront rather than tying medical costs to the individual patient makes sense. The same logic applies in other areas of health care. Most tests and scans are expensive because of patent protection, not because the resources actually used in the process are costly. Once the equipment or testing method has been developed, the value of the resources (labor and materials) used in the test is relatively small. Society must pay for the research and development costs, but these costs have already been paid at the point where an insurer must decide whether to pay for a test for a particular patient.

Some aspects of medical care may always be expensive. Open-heart surgery, involving many hours of the time of highly skilled surgeons, will inevitably carry a substantial price tag. However, once developed, MRI, sophisticated tests for various diseases, or more effective drugs for treating cancer should be available at their marginal cost. The hard decision should be which areas of research to pursue, not whether to withhold potentially life-saving care that in reality costs society very little.

Economists overlook their price-equals-marginal-cost mantra when it comes to the health care sector. They also forget their commitment to globalization and the removal of trade barriers.

This is surprising since one of the most obvious indictments of the U.S. health care system is that its costs are so hugely out of line with costs in the rest of the world—with no corresponding benefits in outcomes. Canada, Germany, France, and the United Kingdom all pay roughly half as much per person for their health care as the United States, yet all these countries, and many more, enjoy longer life expectancies. International comparisons of quality are difficult, but the gap in life expectancies makes it hard to believe that the health care system in the United States is qualitatively better than its peers. Since other countries operate their health care systems far more efficiently, there are enormous potential gains to the U.S. economy in opening this sector to increased international trade.

The health care sector can be opened to global competition in three obvious ways: increasing opportunities for foreign-born medical personnel to work in the United States; facilitating "medical tourism," so that Americans can more easily have major medical procedures performed in other countries; and allowing Medicare beneficiaries to buy into the lower-cost health care systems of other wealthy countries.

Each of these offers enormous opportunities for savings in the health care sector and benefits for the economy. And we can structure any new arrangements to ensure that our trading partners also reap the rewards. This is especially important in the case of developing countries: we cannot let health care savings for the United States come at the expense of reduced access to care for people in the developing world.

Increasing the openness of the United States to highly trained medical personnel should be on every trade economist's mind. Doctors in the United States, especially highly trained specialists, earn far more than their counterparts in Western Europe or Canada, at least in part because it is very difficult for doctors—even those who meet our high standards—to train in other countries and then work in the United States. Licensing procedure acts as a trade barrier.

What if, however, the government sought to remove the barriers for foreign physicians in the same way that it sought in NAFTA to remove barriers for imported goods manufactured in Mexico? Low tariffs were only a small part of the story; for most goods, tariffs were already low. NAFTA's innovation was to promote the transfer of manufacturing facilities to Mexico for the purpose of exporting the output back to the United States. U.S. trade negotiators sat down with manufacturing company executives and asked them about the obstacles to setting up factories in Mexico. They then negotiated a treaty that removed the obstacles.

Similarly, U.S. trade officials can sit down with major hospitals and ask what prevents them from hiring doctors from Mexico, India, and other developing countries at much lower wages than U.S.-born doctors receive. Some impediments are obvious. A hospital cannot legally hire a foreign doctor at a wage that is far below the market rate without first attempting to hire a U.S. citizen or green-card holder at the current market rate. Such protectionist barriers could be easily eliminated. After all, the economic argument for hiring foreign doctors who are willing to work for lower wages than their U.S. counterparts is the same as the argument for buying foreign-made clothing that is cheaper than U.S.-made clothing. The benefits to consumers are clear in both cases.

Drafting international training and licensing standards would be the next step. Doctors could be tested by U.S.-certified testers in their home countries to determine whether they meet the standards. Those who do would have the same opportunities to work in the United States as a U.S. citizen. A kid growing up in Mexico City or Beijing would have as much opportunity to work as a neurosurgeon in the United States as a kid growing up on Long Island.

Compensation in the most highly paid medical specialties averages far above $250,000 a year, even after physicians have paid for their malpractice insurance. Many doctors trained outside the United States would find these positions attractive even if they paid $100,000 a year. Opening medical practice to foreign competition would allow for the same sorts of gains from trade that we have seen with opening trade in apparel and textiles—except that we spend far more on doctors each year than we do on clothes.

In addition, we could impose a fee structure on foreign-trained physicians working in the

United States. The money would go toward compensating their home countries for the cost of their education. This would be comparable to the sort of income-based student loan repayment system that the United Kingdom has put in place. For example, a 10 percent tax would almost certainly support the training of two or more doctors in most developing countries and could ensure that developing countries sending doctors to the United States would also see an improvement in the quality of care at home.

Increased openness in the provision of medical services can lead to other win-win situations. One already exists but lacks government oversight: medical tourism. Facilities in developing countries such as Thailand and India can perform many major medical procedures at costs far lower than prevail in the United States, and for some of these medical procedures the savings of foreign care can easily cover the cost of airfare and hotel bills for the patient and several family members. These facilities are designed to meet Western standards of care; in many cases they are equipped with the most modern medical equipment.

Medical tourism is growing rapidly, and nothing short of a massive overhaul of the U.S. health care system will stop it. U.S. policy-makers should embrace rather than ignore it. They could allow for a huge expansion of medical tourism by certifying facilities in other countries to ensure the quality of care and establishing guidelines for liability in the case of medical malpractice or other issues. Insurance companies could contract with facilities in the developing world and offer large discounts to patients who opt to have major procedures performed in these facilities. Some insurance companies have already offered such options, but the process will advance far more quickly if appropriate institutional and legal structures are put in place.

The U.S. government can also insist that developing countries impose taxes on medical tourism; the proceeds would support improvements in their own health care systems. It will, of course, be difficult to enforce a government's commitment to improving the quality of health care for its citizens if it does not face domestic pressure as well. But, with formal agreements, some revenue from medical tourism will more likely be put to this use.

Finally, why not allow Medicare beneficiaries to buy into the health care system of other countries? Tens of millions of current or future Medicare beneficiaries have close family or emotional ties to countries with more efficient health care systems. At present, however, Medicare beneficiaries moving to these countries cannot apply their Medicare to the provision of health care. They would be left to make health care arrangements for themselves. Retirees have already largely paid for their Medicare benefits through the Medicare payroll tax that they paid when they were working. It seems reasonable that retirees should be allowed to apply the value of this benefit in whatever country they choose to live.

As an incentive for other countries, the U.S. government could offer a premium to countries that allow Medicare beneficiaries to be covered under their health care systems—say, 10 percent above per-person health care costs there. Medicare beneficiaries and the U.S. government could split the savings, which would be substantial. For example, a beneficiary moving to the Netherlands or the United Kingdom in 2010 could expect to pocket close to $2,000 a year from their share of the savings. The amount will grow over time, especially if the explosive projected increases in U.S. health care costs prove accurate. By 2040 beneficiaries may be pocketing more than $8,000 a year (in 2009 dollars) by buying into the health care systems in one of the Western European countries. By 2080 annual savings could reach $30,000 (also in 2009 dollars).

Making this option available could allow Medicare beneficiaries to enjoy much more comfortable retirements and generate enormous savings for the U.S. government. To establish quality control and to give developing countries such as Mexico incentives to improve their health care systems, the program could require that eligible countries have longer life expectancies than the United States. Every country in Western Europe and a few in Eastern Europe would already qualify. Even Jordan could participate.

The goal of course is not to have globe-trotting Americans in search of health care; we should fix the U.S. health care system to provide quality health care at a reasonable price. In the meantime, good policy would take advantage of the potential benefits of using efficient foreign health care systems. Moreover, the competition may well increase the pressure for reform by making the inefficiencies of the U.S. system more apparent. And the global market in medical services might put downward pressure on prices in the United States. If the gap between the cost of major medical procedures performed in the United States and other countries continues to grow, relatively few people might have those procedures performed in the United States. Highly paid medical specialists will either accept lower fees or go with much less work. The same logic will apply to other high-cost areas of the U.S. health care system.

ECONOMISTS, OFTEN PAINFULLY DOGMATIC in pushing economic principles in contexts where they are not appropriate, behave the opposite way in the health care debate: they fail to raise their most basic principles in an arena where they offer enormous potential gains. Economists should act like economists in assessing health care, where the benefits of marginal-cost pricing are even greater than in apparel or cars. And the gains are not only economic. Many of the tough choices created by the current system disappear if patients and their families face only the marginal cost—the actual cost to society—for medical procedures and treatments.

Similarly, economists' commitment to free trade should not end at the hospital door. Globalization offers enormous opportunities: it allows Americans to escape a broken health care system and generates new pressures to fix it. We can structure arrangements that ensure our trading partners benefit as well.

Despite poor management throughout the markets in recent years, sound, mainstream economics is still safe and effective. Health care policy could use a dose.

3

The Big Bank Theory

WALL STREET BANKERS, ALONG WITH the rest of the players in the financial industry, like to think of themselves as swashbuckling capitalists. They battle cutthroat competition with one hand and oppressive government bureaucracy with the other. In reality, however, the financial industry is deeply dependent on the government. Far from the rugged, go-it-alone types they wish they were, they are more like well-dressed, coddled adolescents. And this is true in good times and bad.

The industry's dependency takes five main forms:

1. the explicit safety net provided by government deposit insurance;

2. the implicit safety net provided by "too big to fail";

3. the special privilege of being the only untaxed casino;

4. the invitation to raid state and local governments for fees;

5. the right to change contract terms after the fact.

These dependencies are entrenched, and, despite loud protests to the contrary, the removal of government from the financial sector is not really on the agenda. The industry wants government regulation, just not in a way that curtails its profits. As we have already seen, the issue is not and never has been the free market versus government regulation. The real question in financial regulation is whether regulation will be structured in a way that advances the public interest or in a way that allows the financial sector to prosper at the expense of the rest of us.

PERHAPS THE MOST IMPORTANT FINANCIAL reform to come out of the Great Depression was federal deposit insurance under the supervision of the Federal Deposit Insurance Corporation (FDIC). The FDIC protects banks from the sort of runs that led to the bank failures of that era.

Banks typically keep only a small portion of their customers' deposits on reserve, and, even then, lend most of it at interest. This practice is reasonable because customers are unlikely to want all of their money at the same time. In fact, there may be as much money deposited as withdrawn on any given day.

But if depositors become concerned about the health of the bank, they may rush to pull money out. Those at the bank first will be able to get their money. Later arrivals will be out of luck, as the bank's reserves will be depleted. Thus, before federal deposit insurance, runs were a logical response to the fear of bank failure.

The FDIC completely changes that logic. By insuring the bank's deposits, the FDIC eliminates the incentive for depositors to rush to withdraw their money. They know that their funds (up to the insured level) are safe.

The FDIC lent an enormous amount of stability to the system, and the benefits are shared by depositors and banks alike. However, government insurance means that the market does not offer the normal discipline against risky behavior. Typically, a bank making high-risk loans must offer high interest rates in order to assuage wary depositors. But if the bank has government insurance, depositors need not worry about losing their money thanks to others' unpaid loans. Thus, insurance allows the bank to attract deposits at relatively low interest rates and still incur high risk on loans. If a bank is in financial trouble and has little of its own capital at stake, the incentive to take large risks is even greater. And its customers, who are covered by deposit insurance, have no reason to be concerned about the soundness of a bank, even if the bank ends up suffering large losses and going out of business.

The government, as the insurer, must actively regulate insured institutions so that they do not take advantage of FDIC protection. The response to the Savings and Loans (S&Ls) crisis in the 1980s is a textbook example of what can happen when the government ignores this regulatory responsibility. Heading into that decade, thousands of S&Ls were essentially insolvent. Instead of shutting them down—the customary response to insolvent banks—the Reagan administration encouraged them to earn their way back to solvency. Many, logically, took large risks with insured deposits. In fact, they flaunted their access to deposit insurance by offering higher interest than their competitors in order to attract more money and grow more quickly. As a result, losses more than quadrupled over the decade, eventually costing taxpayers more than $120 billion ($190 billion in current dollars).

The story of the S&Ls is not a free-market one. It is a case of banks ripping off taxpayers. They were not just stealing, they were exploiting the deposit insurance system, thus making government complicit. The lesson is simple: if the government insures the bank's deposits, then it must also regulate the bank. Where the government grants insurance without oversight, banks take big risks at taxpayers' expense.

In addition to monitoring risk-taking at FDIC-insured banks, the government is required to enforce minimum capital-reserve requirements. Together, these safeguards ensure that the banks' shareholders will suffer the first losses. Only then will shareholders try to prevent the bank from making overly risky bets.

Maintaining a minimum level of capital is a difficult regulatory task. At any given time, banks have a wide variety of loans on their books. Some of these loans may be worth only a fraction of their original value, as is the case with many commercial and residential mortgages today. In principle, banks should mark these loans down to their true value so that their books represent ongoing profitability accurately and their balance sheets reflect true net worth. However, banks have little incentive to write down a bad loan before absolutely necessary—showing a loss on their books is bad for stock prices and executive bonuses. Delaying write-downs also allows banks to misrepresent their capital position. If a bank has losses equal to 10 percent of its assets (the standard capital reserve requirement), then it has no real capital, since an accurate accounting would show that the loan losses wipe out their assets. Only if regulators oversee banks' behavior on an on-going basis will banks disclose the true value of their bad loans.

An insured bank must be a regulated bank; there is no way around this. An unregulated bank with government insurance has a license to rip off taxpayers. Unfortunately, many banks have just such a license. In particular, recent rule changes that allow banks to use "fair value" accounting instead of market accounting in assessing the value of their assets enable banks to bury large losses.

Some argue that because deposit insurance is paid for by banks it is not a subsidy and thus should be left unregulated. This is true in normal times, although not in the extreme cases like the S&L crisis, and quite likely will not prove to be true in the current crisis. But even in normal times, when FDIC insurance does not act as a subsidy, the system needs regulation. If the government backed off regulation while still offering insurance, as it did with the S&Ls and is doing to some extent now in allowing fair-value accounting, the losses and therefore the cost of the insurance would skyrocket. The low-risk actors in the industry would bear the costs of the risky behavior of others and, in the end, the system of insurance become unworkable, as happened with the S&Ls.

Even if deposit insurance is privately provided, as is the case in some countries, government involvement is still necessary. Any insurance system that covers a large share of a country's deposits has the implicit backing of the national government in the event of a crisis. No one would believe that the government would let a private insurer collapse if the simultaneous failure of many banks left it insolvent. The private insurer would be acting with an implicit government guarantee. This guarantee would entail regulation in order to prevent abuse.

FDIC OFFERS BANKS AN EXPLICIT SAFETY net. Several large institutions also enjoy an implicit safety net because they are too big to fail (TBTF). This safety net allows them to borrow money (other than insured deposits) at a lower interest rate than would otherwise be the case because lenders know that the government will back up the institutions' loans if necessary.

The implicit TBTF guarantee has become explicit in the current crisis: the government stepped in to back up debts to creditors when Bear Stearns, Fannie Mae, Freddie Mac, and AIG became insolvent. The government had no legal obligation to honor any of the debts incurred by these companies. It justified the intervention by claiming that failure to act would cause serious damage to the financial system and the economy.

The TBTF guarantee extends well beyond this list of failed institutions. Citigroup and Bank of America would almost certainly have faced insolvency had it not been for the extraordinary measures taken by the government to support them in late 2008 and early 2009. Their status even now is questionable, with both banks operating with government guarantees for hundreds of billions of dollars of bad assets. The 2008 Troubled Asset Relief Program (TARP), coupled with access to a special FDIC loan-guarantee program and Federal Reserve lending facilities, kept several other large and troubled financial institutions alive through the worst months of the financial crisis.

In other words, the implicit TBTF guarantee is real. After it allowed the huge investment bank Lehman Brothers to collapse, the government virtually promised that it would not allow another major financial institution to fail. Other large financial institutions took the promise seriously.

What is wrong with that? Because lenders knew that their loans to Goldman Sachs, Citigroup, Morgan Stanley, and other giants were effectively backed by the government, they offered these companies substantially lower interest rates than they offered smaller banks. While large financial institutions are always able to get funds at a somewhat lower cost than smaller institutions, the gap in the cost of funds between small and large banks grew by half a percentage point following the collapse of Lehman. Multiplied by the assets of these institutions, the increase amounts to a $33 billion-a-year subsidy at the expense of small institutions.

There is no reason to allow banks to reach the size of the TBTF institutions. Research on size and efficiency in the banking sector usually shows that all economies of scale can be fully realized at around $50 billion in assets—one twentieth the size of the biggest U.S. banks. That banks in the United States and elsewhere have grown far larger than this may be an indication of the benefits of greater market power, political power, and, of course, the advantage of the TBTF subsidy itself.

Subsidizing the largest financial institutions to the detriment of their smaller competitors is not a free-market policy. Two options could restore the balance: break up the large banks so that they are not recognized as TBTF, or impose regulatory penalties, such as larger reserve requirements, that roughly offset the benefits of the TBTF guarantee. If some banks voluntarily break themselves up into smaller units to avoid the penalty, then we will know that the penalties are comparable in size to the implicit subsidy of TBTF.

SUPPOSE THE STATE OF NEVADA WAIVED the 6.75 percent tax on gambling revenues for one casino in Las Vegas. That casino could promise better odds than its competitors and still have a larger profit margin. Wall Street financial institutions essentially enjoy this kind of advantage: they can profit from gambling opportunities unencumbered by the taxes paid on other forms of gambling.

Not all investment is gambling, of course, but most short-term trades, which comprise the vast majority of trading volume, are comparable. The payoff on a bet on an oil future or credit default swap is, to a large extent, random. Research may help Wall Street traders make informed bets, but it helps serious gamblers at the horse races too. A gambler who knows the stakes is still a gambler. Yet the racetrack gambler will pay 3-6 percent in taxes on her bet, and the Wall Street gambler pays none.

I use the term "gambling" seriously. Gambling may have a financial upside for the gambler, but it provides no benefit to the economy.

If the gambler is successful—as a skilled poker player may be—he is simply taking wealth from others, not adding wealth to the economy. Short-term financial gains are similar.

A long-term investor, however, can rightfully claim that he is providing capital to businesses that increase societal wealth. And a successful long-term investor, such as Warren Buffet, can point to many cases in which his capital allowed companies to grow. These companies presumably provide goods and services valued by society and create jobs. Of course, there are cases in which a company's growth may not be beneficial to society on the whole, but the point remains that long-term investment has the potential to benefit the economy by creating wealth.

Short-term speculation is unlikely to have this effect. For example, if a speculator correctly bets that oil futures will rise in price, she will have captured some of the gain that would have otherwise gone to the producer, which could have sold its product at a higher price. The speculator will probably also have imposed some cost on the purchaser (either an end user or another speculator) who will likely have to pay a higher price in the future than if the speculator had not been an actor in the market.

Speculators can help stabilize markets by forcing prices to adjust more quickly. But "noise traders," who act largely on rumors and focus on anticipating the behavior of other actors rather than fundamentals of supply and demand, impose a cost to the economy by moving prices away from the levels that the fundamentals suggest, thereby destabilizing markets. They make markets give out the wrong signals. If ungrounded speculation drives up a price for oil futures, oil producers might initiate drilling in areas where they will not be able to cover the extraction cost when oil prices return to a non-inflated level. The oil companies will incur losses, and the economy as a whole will suffer a waste of resources.

Distinguishing noise trading from trades based on an assessment of fundamentals is not simple. But, as a general rule, short-term trades fall into the noise-trading category more often than do longer-term trades.

If the government sought to level the playing field across casinos, it could impose a modest tax on each financial transaction. Such a tax would disproportionately affect noise trading, since short-term traders make more transactions than long-term investors. And it could lead to more efficient markets. Not only would fewer resources be wasted in carrying through the financial transactions that support the real economy, but we might see prices that more closely reflect the fundamentals of the market.

In spite of being promoted by some of the world's most prominent economists, such as

Nobel laureates James Tobin and Joseph Stiglitz, financial-transaction taxes have not been put on the agenda in Congress. Tax proposals have been raised far more often since the fall 2008 bailout, but the industry has moved aggressively to squash any serious discussion of the per-transaction tax.

STATE AND LOCAL GOVERNMENTS NEED A wide variety of financial services. The big actors in the industry recognize this fact and promote their products to state and local government officials who often have little understanding of the services they are buying.

In many ways the marketing of financial-service products parallels the defense-procurement process: the contract and bidding systems are often shrouded in secrecy, and products and services are rarely standardized, so prices cannot be easily compared. In this environment political connections are extremely valuable—they often determine whose bid wins a contract. Just as defense contractors spend large amounts of money on lobbyists with close ties to key members of Congress or the military, the financial industry spends large amounts of money developing close ties to key officials in state and local governments. These governments hire financial-sector firms for pension-fund management, financing long-term investments such as school and road construction, and even managing the flow of spending and tax receipts. All of these subcontracted activities offer the financial industry large opportunities for profit and breed corruption.

The current value of state and local pension funds is $2.4 trillion, with management fees and transaction costs averaging 1-2 percent a year. The revenue generated from these funds for the financial industry is in the range of $25 billion to $50 billion a year—most of it a gift from taxpayers. Pension officials could simply put their money in a large index fund, such as Vanguard, whose mix of stocks closely tracks the overall stock market. The administrative cost of keeping money in Vanguard's main index funds is typically about 0.15 percent annually; the difference in cost for state and local governments in managing their money would be $20-$45 billion a year.

The industry has also earned substantial fees selling state and local governments complex financial products inappropriate for public buyers. Typically, if a state or local government wants to finance a major project, it issues a long-term bond, locking in an interest rate for perhaps 10-30 years. This way it can gradually accumulate the money needed to repay its debt. Over the last decade, however, several major investment banks made large sums selling "auction-rate securities" to these governments.

Instead of locking in a long-term interest rate, an auction-rate security breaks up the longer period into a series of short-term loans, typically 30-90 days in duration. At the end of each period, the bond is effectively refinanced for another period. The logic is that the short-term interest rate is generally lower than the long-term interest rate, so a bond financed through successive 30 or 90 day loans may require lower interest payments than ten-year or 30-year bonds.

In 2003 J.P. Morgan Chase used this argument to sell auction-rate securities to Jefferson County, Alabama. It also paid a bribe of $235,000 to Larry Langford, the president of the County Commission at the time. When interest rates subsequently increased, raising the cost of borrowing through auction-rate securities, J.P. Morgan tried to extract a $647 million fee from the county in order to excuse it from its contract. Since the bribe became public and led to a criminal conviction of Mr. Langford, Jefferson County was able to get out of this contract without paying the termination fee.

The school district of Erie, Pennsylvania had similar dealings with J.P. Morgan. The district was persuaded in 2003 to sell complex derivative instruments called "swaptions" with the promise of $750,000 that could be used upfront for school repairs. A swaption is essentially a bet on interest rates, with the seller taking the risk. Three years later, when interest rates took an unexpected turn, the Erie school district had to pay J.P. Morgan $2.9 million to get out of its commitments. A total of 107 Pennsylvania school districts became involved in the swaption business.

These sorts of deals have become common for J.P. Morgan and other major banks. They have earned billions of dollars in fees selling derivative instruments to governments. In many instances the associated fees have little to do with markets. Large firms are preying on governments and, thereby, taxpayers. It is not clear that any of the reform proposals currently being considered by Congress will put an end to this practice.

In our daily lives, we regularly enter into business relationships that have the character of long-term contracts. For example, most families have cable and phone service, and they pay for them on a monthly basis. Service providers, can, and often do, change the terms of these contracts. In the cases of phone, cable, and other public utilities that are subject to government regulation, changes in the terms of contracts often require the approval of a regulatory agency, which, in turn, usually requires that clear notice be given to consumers. There is no such regulation in the financial industry.

The financial industry now draws much of its income from fees and penalties charged to customers who are late with credit card payments or overdraw their checking accounts. Banks are expected to earn $38.5 billion in 2009 on overdraft fees on debit cards and checking accounts and another $20.5 billion on credit card penalties. In 2007 these fees and penalties represented almost 20 percent of the sector's before-tax profits.

In many cases customers were either not aware of the fees or they did not realize how damaging they would be. Customers are frequently charged fees about which they have never been clearly notified. For example, it is now standard practice for banks to provide overdraft protection on debit cards, whereby the bank will cover the cost of a purchase even if it exceeds the money available in the customer's account. The fee is typically six to ten dollars, so debit-card users may find themselves paying a six-dollar overdraft fee to buy a two-dollar cup of coffee. Since few people would make this purchase knowing the fees involved, the banks obviously rely on their customers's lack of awareness about the fee. Legislation passed by Congress in the summer of 2009 requires clear notification of the fees charged on checking accounts and credit and debit cards, although it provides the banks with nine month's grace time, during which they can continue their current practices.

Prior to this legislation, the financial industry had a green light to change unilaterally the terms of long-term contracts in a manner enormously costly for their customers. The change notification might have taken the form of a short letter or paragraph included with advertising and other items and written in language likely to confuse anyone who does not work in finance. The government tolerates this kind of deception in few, if any, other industries. There is no reason—apart from the power of the financial industry—that rate increases or changes in terms for credit cards or bank accounts should be any less clear than the notifications required of utilities.

The recent legislation should limit the extent to which banks can change terms of their contracts in deceptive and ad hoc ways. While this is viewed as government regulation by the banking industry and its allies, in other sectors of the economy, parties do not generally have the ability to change contracts unilaterally. Congress is merely attempting to restore familiar contract law to the sector.

As non-standard as bank fees and penalties may seem, they do not even approach the level of exceptionalism ensured by the bankruptcy reform that the industry pushed through Congress in 2005. The central purpose of the bill was to make it more difficult for individuals to have debts reduced or eliminated through bankruptcy. The industry successfully framed proponents as enforcers of contracts, while the opponents, supposedly, wanted to excuse borrowers who were down on their luck.

But lenders, who had poorly judged credit risk, could just as easily be accused of running to the government for help in collecting their debts. The banks presumably understood the risk that they were taking in making loans in the first place. They are in the business of distinguishing good credit risks from bad. A financial institution that is unable to make such distinctions is misallocating capital. The economy would benefit if it went out of business.

But the bankruptcy reform went the other way, involving the government more deeply in the debt-collection process, thereby increasing the value of the bad loans issued by banks and other lenders. The new law did not just apply to debt assumed after 2005, but retroactively. Borrowers who had taken out credit card debt–loans under one set of bankruptcy rules were faced with a different, stricter, set of rules if they eventually fell on economic hardship. Again, not a story of the free market. This is a transfer of wealth from debtors to creditors—yet another case where the banks used their political power to override market outcomes.

THE DEBATE OVER REGULATION IN THE financial industry has been badly distorted. The government must be directly involved in the operation of the industry, most obviously through deposit insurance, but also through many other channels. No one in this debate really advocates an end to government regulation. Industry advocates want to end or weaken regulations that reduce their profits, but they are not willing to end the government supports that make their profit and survival possible.

The debate must be returned to appropriate grounds: a question of how best to structure regulation, not a question of regulation versus the market. Which regulations structure the financial industry so that it will serve the larger economy? This means providing incentives for the industry to better serve consumers and investors, rather than providing incentives to prey on them. There should not be large returns for writing deceptive contracts. Nor should short-term speculation be the most effective way to get rich.

The economy thrived in the three decades following World War II with a financial sector that was proportionately one-fourth of its current size. There is no reason that the financial sector should use up a larger share of the economy's resources today than it did three decades ago. Effective regulation will restore the financial sector to its proper role in the economy.

4

An Economy for Everyone

PROGRESSIVES HAVE PAINTED THEM-selves into a corner by accepting a policy debate in which they are on one side and the market is on the other. This framing is both essentially wrong and a bad political move. Progressives must recognize that "market fundamentalism" does not exist. Conservative restructuring of the economy, not the natural workings of the market, caused the upward redistribution of income and wealth during the last three decades. Progressives must always point out ways in which conservatives use the government to bring about their desired outcomes.

Still, while progressives should support government interventions that are needed in order to level the playing field, they should not view an increased role for government as an end in itself. The idea of government bureaucrats directing major areas of the economy and individuals' lives does not generally resonate well with Americans.

Thinking clearly about the roles of the government and the market may lead progressives in unexpected directions. The best solutions will often involve a greater role for the market. This is certainly the situation with prescription drugs, where government-granted patent monopolies have turned a product that is inherently cheap into one that can be incredibly expensive for consumers. The result is exactly what economic theory predicts: enormous amounts of rent-seeking and corruption. We end up paying thousands of dollars for drugs that would cost a few dollars per prescription in a free market, and we cannot trust either the research or our doctors, because we know that experts may be influenced by drug company payments. The solution—the economic arrangement that advances societal well-being—in this case lies with the market, and progressives should happily embrace this path.

Policy debates affect more than economic outcomes. The ability to structure markets hugely influences the course of future politics. For example, trade policies that put unionized manufacturing workers in direct competition with low-wage labor in the developing world enormously weakened the labor movement in the United States. Deregulation in trucking, airlines, and telecommunications undermined some very strong unions in these sectors—and their political power as well.

In principle, progressives can design policies that not only produce immediate economic benefits but also improve the prospects for progressive politics in the long term. Health care is a case in point. If drug companies could no longer rely on patent monopolies, they would have less influence in Congress and state legislatures. If doctors faced more direct competition from those trained in other countries, then the doctors' lobbies might be less effective in pushing their agendas. Weakening a group's economic power also reduces its political power. The right understands this basic fact very well. Progressives must learn it.

If the political obstacles to an economy that serves the majority of Americans are enormous, so are the potential benefits. Following World War II, the United States enjoyed three decades of rapid growth, with gains broadly shared. With the right policies in place, the economy can return to this sort of growth. Dismantling the regulations that produced upward distribution and recovering their accompanying waste would offer real gains to those for whom the riches of the boom years proved elusive.

Consider this: if the share of GDP devoted to health care fell from the current 17 percent to the 10 percent typical of the next-most expensive set of health care systems, more than $900 billion a year would be available for other uses. That is $3,000 per American. There would be comparable, if somewhat smaller, benefits from redirecting the financial system toward efficiency rather than quick, massive profits.

We have paid a big price as a country for the political turn to the right over the last three decades. There are huge potential gains in reversing the course.

ACKNOWLEDGMENTS

THE ARGUMENTS IN THIS BOOK HAVE BENefited from numerous discussions over the years with friends and colleagues. In particular, Eileen Appelbaum, Heather Boushey, Helene Jorgensen, David Rosnick, John Schmitt, and Mark Weisbrot have provided much useful feedback over the years. Deborah Chasman and Simon Waxman gave me many helpful comments and did an outstanding job editing my writing. They also deserve credit for the suggestion to bring these essays together as a book. I thank Helene, Kiwi, and Walnut for their patience, as I neglected them to focus on this and other work.

BOSTON REVIEW BOOKS

Boston Review Books is an imprint of *Boston Review*, a bimonthly magazine of ideas. The book series, like the magazine, is animated by hope, committed to equality, and convinced that the imagination eludes political categories. Visit bostonreview.net for more information.